Underground
Musicians

Underground Musicians

Carol Coffee Reposa

LAMAR UNIVERSITY Press

ISBN: 978-0-9850838-0-9
Library of Congress Control Number: 2013944474

Manufactured in the United States

Lamar University Press
Beaumont, Texas

Acknowledgments

The author gratefully acknowledges the following journals and anthologies in which some of these poems first appeared.

Amarillo Bay
anniversary di verse city
Anthology of Magazine Verse &
    Yearbook of American Poetry
Atlanta Review
Blue Hole
Blue Mesa Review
Borderlands
CCTE Studies
The Chaffin Journal
Coal City Review
Concho River Review
Context South
descant
a di.verse.city odyssey
di.verse.city too
English in Texas
English Journal
The Enigmatist
The Formalist
Green Hills Literary Lantern
Inlet
Iron Horse Literary Review
Journal of Texas Women Writers
Langdon Review

New Texas
Palo Alto Review
Pecan Grove Review
Quirk
Revista/Review Interamericana
Right Hand Pointing
RiverSedge
Roanoke Review
The Same
San Antonio Current
San Antonio Express-News
San Pedro River Review
Scholarship and Creativity On
    Line: A Journal of the Texas
    College English Association
Sustaining Abundant Life,
    Women's Prayer and Poetry
The Texas Observer
Texas Poetry Calendar
Valparaiso Review
Voices
Voices de la Luna
Windhover
Windows

Poetry from Lamar University Press:

Alan Berecka, *With Our Baggage*
David Bowles, *Flower, Song, Dance*: Aztec *and Mayan*
    Poetry (a new translation)
Jeffrey DeLotto, *Voices Writ in Sand*
Mimi Ferebee, *Wildfires and Atmospheric Memories*
Michelle Hartman, *Disenchanted and Disgruntled*
Dave Oliphant, *The Pilgrimage, Selected Poems: 1962-2012*

For information on these and other Lamar University Press books go to

www.LamarUniversityPress.Org

Other Books by Carol Coffee Reposa

At the Border: Winter Lights
The Green Room
Facts of Life

For Emily, Ethan, Jonah, Connor, and Cash,
the five blazing sputniks

CONTENTS

III. Otherworldly Red: Russia

IV. A Web of Green: Home

I. Gold Hibiscus: Mexico, Peru, and Ecuador

Flashback

One ordinary morning
I sit at my desk
Bills and tax forms
Ranged before me
In their unforgiving stacks.
I note vacantly
The dark blue print of someone's letterhead

And twenty years
Are gone.
It's midnight
And I'm back in Mazatlán
Floating in a pool
Blue water
Laced with red hibiscus.
Marimbas in the background
Shimmer through the dark
Like raindrops
In the darkest sky I've ever seen
Obsidian
Broken only
By the blazing stars
Burning, spinning
While I drift through flowers
All those old, relentless lights.

A jangling phone
Drops in the scented waters
And I fall back
Into morning
Like a tired red star
Hibiscus petals
Floating past my hands.

Colors of the Mexican Coast

Hunger is the shade
Of lemon sherbet
Or a slice of watermelon.

People speak in tones
Of mango or papaya
Dispute a price

In iridescent red like parrots' plumes
Their voices hard
As scales on an iguana.

Sweat ripens in the lanky palms
Like coconuts
Glazes streets in pale green drops

Or burns
In orange flames
Like blossoms on a jacaranda.

A child grows up
In broken cinderblocks
Blue as the rivers

He has never seen
One mile from a banana palace,
Glass-topped walls as bright

As white paint
On the trunks of trees.
Later, in a turquoise dusk

Tiles fall from roofs
In streams of cinnabar.
Then night swirls in, black

And pierced with stars
Before the colors
Start again.

Dancing in Veracruz

Sweat pours down us all
Like warm rain
Beneath a giant palapa

Our unaccustomed gringo feet
Tangled in the rhythms
Of a mariachi, a fandango

As we celebrate a birthday
Flying to the beat
Of the river just beyond.

We whirl to the pulse of trumpets
And guitars, twang of the *jarana*
Faster, faster

Voladores from the North
Spinning, almost weightless
As the song moves toward its end

And we collapse
In steamy laughter
By the Boca del Rio
Flowing, flowing
Past us all.

At Parque Museo La Venta

At the gate
A toddler floats on her quilt
Like a small statue
While her mother
And the other vendors
Spread their painted wares
On colored blankets
Turning dust to red and green
Like petals fallen
From a giant flower.

Inside
The Olmec faces
Gaze at us inscrutably
Their granite eyes blank as walls
Under heavy lids twelve inches wide
Their heads five feet across
Mouths in a timeless sulk
Features drooping
Under weight
We can not guess.

We leave.
At the gate
The toddler still sits.
She doesn't move, scarcely blinks
Knows somehow that her world ends
At the border of her quilt
Bright red in the dust,
Like the sculptures inside
Rounded by landscaped mango trees
Their gold fruit
Falling to the ground.

At a Hotel Near Uxmal

Golondrinas swirl
Around the swimming pool
Darting in and out
Of turquoise water
In the steamy half-light
Of late afternoon.

Behind them
Seven models strut
In five-inch heels
Tilt and turn for the camera,
Their shoulders arched
Polished legs and bright bikinis
Catching light
Like moving prisms.

The photographer wants more
So they twirl translucent cover-ups
Around their hips
Toss their golden hair
While shutters snap
And we look on
Shaded by flame trees
In the garden.

At a distance miles beyond us
The giant pyramid glows
White in tangled green
A cipher in the jungle dusk
Gleaming like an alien jewel,
A misplaced queen.

Mayan on the March

Pacheco's mural shows the *indio*'s feet
Nothing but his feet
Their long stride raising clouds of dust
That billow through the gallery.

Calloused, seamed, without shoes
They leave their giant portrait
Walking off the canvas
Straight through me, passing through

Four centuries of hunger in the heat
Weight no one could carry
Thirst never satisfied
Sweat rolling into an early grave

But the *indio* outlasts his journey
Continues his long march
Through deserts, sawtoothed mountains
Boiling coasts

Toward a street
Filled with talk
Marimbas and dappled light
At last cold water in the shade.

Sierra Madre Occidental

A gaunt mother,
Her vast ribs and breasts
Protrude in the shifting light.

Haggard from millennia
Spent watching over everything,
She changes her crumpled dresses constantly

From blue to green
Charcoal to sapphire
Black or sometimes pink

Before she pulls the sky down
Into her giant lap
To rest.

A rough-out dowager
She fosters her millions of children
Forever.

I sleep at her knees.

Love in Another Language
(for Nicho)

I have no words
For the smile
Of a ten-year-old
Who brings me coffee and a *quesadilla*
Or the sobs in a *balada*
Weeping from the radio
Or the guide
Who throws me
From the path of a Corvette
Racing down a narrow street.

No phrase fits
The street parade in Guanajuato,
Músicos strolling down cobbles
Ten guitars smiling in a mountain night.
Nor can I translate
Fields of blue maguey
Rolling down a slope, a misplaced ocean,
Or the *malecón* in Vera Cruz
The sky a glittering hot blanket
Covering the Gulf.

My dictionary offers nothing
For the Sierras all around us
Hovering like watchful mothers,
Or the random songs of windchimes
In a storm. No verb conveys the motion
Of our bus floating through the clouds
In the Tuxtlas. No noun contains
The limestone castles of Palenque,
Emerald sweat in the jungle, *escaleras*
On a pyramid, a Mayan's silent stride.

And when I collapse on a Saltillo street

I can't articulate
The man who drags me to a taxi,
Then the hospital,
Or the flower-like nurse
Who strokes my face,
Preps my arm, finds the vein
Just in time
And sits with me while I dream
Of everything that I can't say.

At the American Embassy in Lima

The young guard
Cradles his longarm
Almost with affection, scans the crowds
Who pass his checkpoint.

Dark beret and camouflage
Stand out before the gray *garúa*
And, beyond, the Andes
Rising like a scream against the sky.

I wonder if he's seen
The polo fields inside the compound
Or the windowless reception room
Beyond those metal doors

Its walls and ceilings
Studded with gold stars
On a phalanx of blue tiles
And bullet-proof glass.

We move slowly through the system
And a row of mute Marines
Up the elevator
To the briefing room.

We sit, take notes, ask questions
At the proper times
But I am thinking
Of the young Peruvian

Outside the walls
One arm around his rifle
And the mountains at his back.

In the Catacombs

We move quickly
Down the darkened flights
Steps rounded, polished
From the footfalls of three centuries

Beneath St. Francis
And his marble world
White lambs
Cradled in his arms

Past the library
Largest in its time
A labyrinth of dust
And crumbling texts

Below the reading room
Where pale friars
Must have squinted
Day and night

Before we reach the first pit
And our guide begins to speak
Flashing his white teeth
Deep dimples and a giant smile.

"This really is the best part."
He points out
The skulls. They rise in gritty heaps
Aimless sockets taking in the dark.

Another excavation
Holds five hundred pelvises.
A third is stuffed with femurs, ulnae
Thin bones of the feet.

"Archeologists are counting
To this day." His gaze heats up
The airless space. I feel his warm breath
On my neck, smell time, desire and faded flesh.

We crouch below damp archways
Grope for the exit
Crowd at last
Into open air
A Moorish courtyard
Redolent of flowers and flowing streams.
I breathe red roses
And the guide says

"Exquisite, don't you think?
This garden honors brothers
Who were martyred
In Japan."

Saturday Night

After a raucous night
Of Spanish vaudeville
Rich with puns and pratfalls
Gags and rolling eyes

We pile into a grimy cab
Leave Magdalena
Heading out
Toward Miraflores.

Taxis bump and grind
Through late-night traffic
And a fog of diesel fumes
Miles of neon, blaring horns.

Then I see
The two of them
Beneath a eucalyptus
In a darkened court.

He's tall and blond.
She's tensile
Like a dancer
In the wings.

He turns to her
And they dissolve
Bodies blurred
In deep green leaves

While midnight crowds
Go by
And music plays
Next door.

I look at them, recall
That old desire, that hunger
To consume
And be consumed.

Costa Verde

A hairpin highway
Snakes along the beach
Along the gray Pacific combers
Humboldt cold, rolling in,

Another and another, day and night
Salt and dingy bubbles
Bursting over miles
Of tires and bottles

Cans and plastic chairs
Refuse of the centuries
In fetid heaps
Swaying with the tide.

Between the breaking waves
Dogs in ribby packs
Scour the steaming hills
Bark at fuming buses as they pass.

I look beyond the steady motion
Wonder what will happen
Out there someday
When the green coast, sea and heaven
Meet.

On the Road to Paracas

I am dreaming
This dun world
Monotone of grayish brown
Sea the same shade as the sky
And mountains just beyond.

Ten miles have passed
Since I last saw
A tinge of green
On anything
Just gray and brown
Salt water, rocks and gritty clouds
A tattered billboard
Hawking Inka Kola...
Later on, a chicken ranch
Dun chickens
In a mist
Of dust
Abiding through this afternoon
And every other

While I try
To think
Of other colors
So removed
I can not spell their names.

Viewing the Nazca Lines

Our single-engine Cessna
Bobs like an oversized cork
In ocean air.

We dip and lurch
Through shaky space
And the world gets small:

Fields and terraces
Shrink into a jigsaw puzzle
Cut in green, gold, brown

Interlock with the Pacific
Glittering like blue lamé.
We climb higher

And the Andes crumple
Like old tissue
Or a mocha cream meringue

Left out on a summer afternoon.
Nothing can prepare us
For the shapes

That jump out suddenly
From dust below:
Eyes that stretch for miles

A parrot's beak
That clamps a cliff
The tail of a spider monkey

Spiraling across the horizon
A giant's hands
Forever raised in prayer.

An ancient dog
Drowns out our humming engine
Barks for centuries.

We fly away
Look back
And they are gone

Somewhere on the gritty plain,
The blue Pacific
Widening before our gaze.

Machu Picchu

The Spaniards never found it
Not a single course of stone
Never saw the solstice
Open over temple walls
Through perfect trapezoids
Their edges carved in light.

A mike clutched in his hand
Our guide explains it all
Inside a wheezing bus.
Our transport lumbers upward
Angles painfully around the unbanked turns
A pregnant woman weary, close to term.

I think about Pizarro's men
Toiling up that steep incline
Their fine Castilian horses
Lathered in the mountain air
Saddle leather molding,
Orchids dangling from strange trees

While water flowed above them
Over stones and terraces
Down green slopes draped in clouds
Like shawls around the shoulders
Of a woman
Lost in thought.

Water streamed out everywhere
Collected in bright pools
Around the condor's head
Dripped in holy mortars
Filled the corners
Of the world.

But in Cusco
Spanish soldiers peeled the gold
From every wall
Filled storage rooms with silver
Smashed pillars of the sun
Slowly strangled Atahualpa.

We finally arrive
Walk the grass still damp from morning rain.
Red poppies sprout
From terrace tops and roofless gables
Gathering light
Like chalices.

Madreselva

The word envelops me:
Jungle mother, mother jungle
Furiously green
Womb of history, labyrinth of ferns
And tendrils inching up my mind.

Too much for the widest lens
She's moving up the Amazon
With parrots, howler monkeys
In her wake
Bromeliads draped around the bridge.

I look out from the prow
See silhouettes on curving banks
Black lines of trees
That grew
Before the Crucifixion.

Her throbbing engine wakes me
And the slick brochure
Falls into the stream
Muddy currents
Bearing it away.

Coca Chewer in a Quito Museum

He's still addicted
After fifteen centuries
That beatific gaze
Caught in time
And non-glare glass.

He cradles a small bowl
Once filled with something
Gods would want
Absolute contentment in his eyes
The tell-tale lump in his jaw

Like a big-league pitcher
Focused on a perfect point
Beyond the catcher
Just before
He throws another strike.

I think of vanished hands,
Careful fingers shaping
Rounding out the terra cotta limbs
To please a pantheon
That gathered somewhere

In the sky or sun or moon.
Track lights catch
The bearer's tranquil face, unblemished
After dusty epochs he spent buried
In the *altiplano*.

As we leave
I almost feel
That old ceramic bowl
In my embrace,
A tell-tale swelling in my jaw.

John Donne at the Equator

He stumbles from the bus to start his search,
Instead sees swirling gray. He thinks of lines
To start a sonnet, outworn laws, old signs:
The earth's sharp corners, ships about to lurch
Into the serpent's jaws, their oak keels perched
Along the edge of ruin, vast teeth like tines
To tear off creaking sails. No science shines
To pull the vessels back, no newfound church.

But now he's striding up the walkway flanked
By granite busts of those who like him knew
This terror was imagined, fruit of loss
And fevered nights, though even these minds ranked
Such learning small when lovers, children drew
Their final breaths, those sighs beneath the Cross.

Playa de Atamari

I almost think I can go back
To those white years.

Without the frigate birds and tamarinds
This might be San Diego
Where I watched lights
Flicker on the mountains
Glide across the harbor
Counted ships as they put out to sea
Inside a ring of tugs
Charcoal queens
Surrounded by their humming drones.

I almost think my parents
Are alive
My sister still a flame
Of copper curls
And purple thoughts.
We are cooking out
Somewhere on Catalina
And my days still stretch before me
Wave on wave.

Then I look out,
See the fury
Of those black Pacific cliffs.
Crags erupt from sand
Like giant teeth,
Tear the rollers
Into boiling lace
White explosions
In an endless line.

Then I know
Just where I am.

Galápagos Soap Opera
(For Ethan)

The cormorants
Are young and restless
Chasing everything on fat webbed feet
Water dripping from their flightless beaks.
Further out
Sea turtles gambol in the waves

Make love a hundred hours at a time.
While they are losing sleep
Father hawks must raise their young alone
Because their faithless mates have flown
To build their blended homes
In foreign *palosanto* trees.

Penguins marry and remarry
At unearthly rates
Waddle through their noisy court dates
As the waves roll in
And the world turns.
Voyeurs in some episodes

Iguanas smolder in their scales.
They have everything it takes
For a menage a trois .
But on a less progressive beach
Sea lions bark and screech
Eight days a week

If even one contender
Flops up on a rock
To plot
His next move on the harem.
In another torrid cove, the sally-lightfoot crabs
Are roundheeled in their quest

To keep up with the albatrosses
Who show off in daily rituals
Of afternoon delight and clattering lust
Tete a tete and beak to beak
While gaggles of blue-footed boobies watch
And sibling rivalry goes unchecked

Around the dinner table
Dotted with abandoned eggs
And empty nests.
Night falls
But just like sands in an hourglass
The sagas

Of these wings and whiskers
Scales and feathers
Glassy eyes and guano
Will continue
On these sunbaked islands
All the days of their lives.

Los Amantes de Sumpa

First she died
And then he died
Ten thousand years ago.

She was twenty.
He was twenty-five.
Both were well off for their time.

Mourners laid him next to her,
Placed his arm around her waist,
His leg across her thigh.

This man and woman
Could have watched
The sun come up each day

In bursts of red and gold
Or listened for the early morning birdsong
While they thatched their roof.

Perhaps they married
Had a feast.
She might have borne a child.

I look at all the tangled bones
His skull crushed
From centuries of earth

Hollows of their eyes
Filled long ago with bright desire
What remains of him still turned to her.

It doesn't matter
When they died
Or why, or how.

All that counts this afternoon
Or any other
Is his arm around her waist,
His leg across her thigh.

Amazonia

Tambopata and La Torre, Madre de Dios:
Their syllables move through my sleep
Like heartbeats.
Waking, dreaming
I am in the jungle now
Our long canoe gliding
On a darkened stream. Maybe we climb
Into the canopy
Black green
Sliced by screeches
An eruption of blue wings
Parrots flying by in iridescent pairs.

I hear nightingales
Inside the long tongues of lianas
See birds of paradise
Lost in strangler figs. Then morning
Forces light between sharp fronds. I wake
To catch the news and weather
Traffic snarled for miles.
I start for work
But at the interchange
Clouds of dark green butterflies
Rise up to block my way. The Southern Cross
Begins to glitter in a vast Pacific night

And now I feel
The warm breath of those rivers:
Tambopata and La Torre, Madre de Dios.

II. Light Bent Blue: Western Europe

Genealogy in Connemara

Roofless gables
Rise like skeletons
Along the road,
Unlikely flowers
Blooming in the gorse.

Stones are everywhere:
Cairns bloom in the bog
Like giant mushrooms
Relics of old grief
Sprouting in the green.

I look for my family
In these fields
Reinvent the plaster, thatch
Peat cut into neat squares
Ponies on the moor

Perhaps a bottle on the table
Tea and bread
A turnip-cutter somewhere
Faces moving through the door
One like mine

Another and another
Threadbare nuns and grizzled priests
Scrawny children with furious red hair
Haggard mothers, punning drunks
A hungry scholar lugging his books

Before the gray swells
Rise, swallow
Everything
And a wet wind
Blows me out to sea.

At Blarney Castle

The rain here is a lens.
We plod through gray refractions
Toward the keep
Light bent into round towers,
Stumble up the narrow spirals
Angled for armored feet.

As we climb, I look at ruined rooms
Rock walls slippery against my hand
Like the lines of a stale seducer,
Patter of a tired comedian.

At last I reach the ramparts
Take in the dripping green of Cork
Its heavy skies
And razor wind.

And now the kiss: attendants lean me back
Into the fable like Rapunzel showing off
A backbend, and my mouth glides down wet stone,
A date gone wrong in all this cold.

They say I'll have the power now
To talk my way through anything.
I think about my grandfather
Who lived here once

Left for Texas and a woman, talked her
Into hunger, years of fights
Battlements of words
And stony wit.

I leave the crenelations
Thinking of the stories
I could tell,

Clever incantations that would guide me
Down these stairs,
A slick descent.

Crossing the English Channel
(for Jim)

Up on the verandah deck
We watch the White Cliffs
And their endless circling gulls,
Dover Castle
And a lighthouse
Receding on the horizon.

I suddenly remember the old song
And think of bluebirds
Fluttering above the rocks
Sunlight on their wings
And music in the air,
An eternal coming home.

Noisy little boys
Arms outstretched
Run along the taffrail
Imitating fighter pilots
While their mothers look out
Behind sunglasses, sip their wine.

Beyond the chirps of pink-cheeked babies,
The patter of bronzed young men
Muscling through their soccer shirts
I begin to hear other sounds: rusty engines
Churning as they crossed to Dunkirk
Rumble of landing craft at Normandy

Staccato chatter of machine-gun fire
Men calling for their mothers.
I see those other youths looking back
On the cliffs, maybe their last glimpse
Of home before Verdun, the Somme, or Omaha Beach
Sailors steeling themselves for Agincourt.

They must have heard the same screeching gulls,
The same muffled swells, seen the same chalk towers
Before they turned away to set their eyes
On a foreign shoreline, everything else
Rolling away
Under blue-gray waves.

At Shakespeare's Birthplace

I buy a magnifier in the shop,
Its handle cast to catch the playwright's shape,
The Bard himself. I grip his pewter chest
And stroke his doublet, run my fingers down
His face, that trademark triangular beard.
If I squeezed hard enough, would protean words
Erupt from my arthritic hand and flow
On fire through my Cross pen as once they did
From his iconic quill? Would my ink dry
To form new plays for the Millennium?
Perhaps I could scrawl magic handkerchiefs
And small beer on my Palm Pilot, or write
A New Age Lear on Twitter, make his heath
A kinder, gentler place. I might at last
Wean Falstaff from his sack and let him see
His knees, rush Hamlet to a therapist
Before he stabbed Polonius, or buy
Two cell phones for the Friar and Romeo.
With luck I might concoct a scent to wash
The blood from Lady Macbeth's hand, create
A perfect Facebook match for Egypt's queen,
The lover not so grand, who would not drive
Her to the fatal asp. Or best of all,
My ipod might contain some food of love
To download for the blue Orsino. Could
I point and click my way to lasting fame?

Such possibilities warm in my hand,
I walk down Henley Street to join the band
Of tourist brothers, breathe iambic air,
Observe poetic dust on my new Crocs
And watch for curtains rising in the crowd.

Elizabeth I on Weaning

While I was yet a child still fidgeting
Through Latin verbs, the lute or virginal,
They told me of my birth. At Greenwich Hall
I first drew breath. My mother tried to bring
Me to her breast, to let her new milk sing
In me but at the King my Father's call
A servant hurried me away, in thrall
Like all the others to his hungering.
And now encased in ermine, shining pearl,
Gold in my hair, an island in my hand,
Surrounded by a swarm of jeweled drones
I still remember thirsting in my bones
And going dry, my tears stopped on command,
A fierce old woman hidden in a girl.

On Her Parents

The King did not admit my birthright, turned
Away when Kat called his attention to
My clothes, just as he never heard the blue
Seas ringing in my mother's laugh. He learned
All tongues with ease and grace, read Greek, discerned
The dark red vintages, but never knew
The iron force of her queenly vows, nor drew
A sigh when suppliant, she trampled ferns
At Greenwich, wept before the court, to plead
A frugal mercy. I was in her arms,
My hair a flame against her breast. But soon
They took her to those darkened rooms. No moon
Shed light along those turrets. No alarms
Were struck. The stones consumed her. Still I bleed.

Death of Edward VI

My sweet consumptive king reigns from his bed,
His face as white and secret as a pearl,
The surface growing slowly in a curl
Of sand enclosed in a lost sea. Hopes fed
On stars and trumpets at his birth are shed
In ink and secret signings or a furl
Of crackling parchment while my prayers still swirl
Before his eyes, lost letters at his head,
Words spent. I know he will recall the fine
Red brick of Hatfield, chrisms carried, long
Bright books, green leaves we read. While God's grace still
Endows his breath, he'll know. Despite the chill
Hands of Northumberland, the hungry throng
Of crowns and thrones, his last words will be mine.

Mary Tudor

Her rosary clicks past her fingers like
My footfall in this cell, sins falling through
The fissures in these cold stones, lost like dew
In morning's dampened light. Those black beads strike
Her nails in steady lockstep, each a spike,
Grim soldiers marching past her fine *pre dieu*
To reach uncertain landmarks framed by rue
Or old rebuffs, each word a whetted pike
Hurled at the open sea. I can't assure
The outcome of these dark devotions, know
what nightingales will sing in these strange wakes.
But where my mother sleeps, I stand. She takes
My fear in her gold hands, whose edges glow
In these lost rooms, whose gestures still endure.

In Exile

I hear the milkmaid singing in the park,
Her fingers roughened by the tugging on
Unwilling cows, while my white hands are fawns
That leap across green meadows past the dark
Iron gates where Bedingfield keeps watch. A lark,
Her wings bound tight, she celebrates each dawn
Her life locked in this mead, while I, the pawn
Of every grasping king, sleep with the mark
Of swords at every door. I hear them through
The satin hangings, echoing along
The gilded ceiling of my room. I weep
For quills and paper, fragile threads to keep
Those voices still. I am denied. The strong
Hands of the milkmaid shine like leaves, like dew.

Leaving the Tower for Her Coronation

My legs grow stiff with this much kneeling, prayers
That cut through purple velvet like the claws
Of ancient lions opening their jaws
To Daniel, turning, pacing in their lairs
In blank desire to have the blood and cares
Of all that does not crouch within the laws
Of amber flanks and manes, the leap that mauls
Before it tears a slender throat. The stares
Of these black stones reach past my days to cries
And whispers, pleas and fragile arms, sounds bent
Into the corners of this cell. But I
Will carry them into the streets. The sky
Will blaze with voices, jewels that weep, the glint
Of cheers and blessings caught in ermine eyes.

Leicester

My Master of the Horse will canter through
This day, and all the days to come. He knows
The pulse beneath my skin, the wind that blows
Behind my eyes. He measures what is true
Among green oaks at Windsor, bill and coo
Of pigeons in the park, the blood that flows
Beyond the stag I killed one year. He sows
The dreams that breathe through time. His hands endue
My hours with brightness cutting through the night.
He's always seen the shadows in my soul,
The moon eclipsed by blood-stained blocks, those thick
Stone battlements that buried hope. The click
Of daggers only speeds his stride, a foal
With shining flanks who leaps toward endless light.

Defeat of the Armada

Spain's raised her swords, but I'll outlast them all.
"I have the heart and stomach of a king,"
I vowed. My fighters cheered, the ring
Of massed deep voices echoing the fall
Of Parma from his armored cliff, the call
Of iron to wood and flesh. It rose to fling
A pebble rippling to Rome, to sling
New tides along French beachfronts, made Spain small.
For them I honor stars, each ragged flame,
Even the fireships staggering across
The Channel in the night like drunks along
Rough cobbles, though I sickened at the strong
Dark smell of blood and drowning horses, loss
Of thought, of all. But still I honor flame.

William Cecil

Burleigh sickens now, his body smaller
Every day in these great rooms. His hands
Stretch further every hour, grope toward lands
He's never seen until his fingers, sure
Of all they grasped in youth--fine quills, the lure
Of parchment moving seas--are lost. He spans
The empty air and drops his spoon. The sands
Recede toward sky. I feed him then, deter
Him in his journey one more day. But he
Has always shuffled what he could not hold
To God: the heavy jeweled kings I shunned,
The crowns I never bore. His hunchback son
will serve me now, his footfall measured, cold
On marble stairs that wind toward memory.

On Her Approaching Death

Outside the branches creak beneath the weight
Of winter and lost leaves, but even this
Sound, all, will soon subside into a hiss
Caught up in time and swept beyond the gate
Of what I know. I can not keep the state
In plenty now. I've sold my jewels. The kiss
Of velvet robes is brutal and remiss.
It cuts my back. I stumble, read my fate
In the gold ring my servants had to break
Because it grew into my hand. The men
At Richmond beg for me to talk. I thirst
And do not speak. My best words burst
Out forty years ago. They made my judges thin:
"Have a care for my people." My hands shake...

The Expulsion of Lucifer, Sistine Chapel

His pallid buttocks
Are all we see of him,
His face turned away
As God hurls him from heaven
In elongated rage

That sweeps through time,
And a lurid sun glowers beyond.
God watches this retreat,
His luminous finger
Pointing the way to ruin.

Lucifer does not yet know
What awaits him,
How he'll darken
Hour by hour
Age by age

Until his thoughts are opaque
As the space around him
And he has no memory
Of light
That he once bore.

Above him
Saints are saved
Prophets speak
The sky stays blue
And God remembers.

Charioteer, Delphi

Children swarm around him.
Tourists hustle
For their cameras
And thousands of shutters
Snap.

He doesn't look at them,
His eyes forever
On the finish line,
A triumph
If he wins.

His horses are beyond him,
Racing
Through some other age
But he is ready
For the start.

A sweat band
Squeezes his carved curls.
He stands serene, barefoot,
His bronze robes draping him
In folds the shade of olive trees.

Missing his left arm
He waits for the signal,
His one hand balancing the reins.
They float toward his vanished horses
Weightless as a falling scarf

While he gazes
Straight ahead
His copper lashes
Still
In that white light.

III. Otherworldly Red: Russia

Learning Cyrillic

I think of that old saint,
His elegant long fingers
Draped around a quill
Faint penumbra glowing on old wood
Cheekbones slanting sharply
In thin light

And I begin to understand
His letters,
Characters that fill the parchment
Stretched like wheat
Across a plain
Or jagged like the Caucasus
Some rounded like gold domes
Of Byzantine cathedrals
Angled like a metropolitan's white beard
Steep verticals like birches
Or a Baltic horizontal
Ending with a flourish
Like the leaps of trepak dancers
Red belts flying in the snow
Or climbing to a shriek
Gaunt as faces
Caught in Leningrad.

Sitting in an air-conditioned room
In Texas,
Seeking shelter from the heat
I start to feel
An ice-edged wind
That slowly melts
To June's white nights, a languid sun
While I approach those final letters
Rising like the Kremlin from the page.

Moscow MTV

The windows of this building
Frame dark comedy
All day, all night.

Forty feet above
Someone throws a table out
Legs spinning

In wild arcs
That end in turbid water
Twenty stories down.

Cassette tape
Floats like streamers
In a vague parade.

Someone rips a pillow
Snowflake feathers
Whirling in a makeshift blizzard

Through the summer afternoon
Large confetti
Celebrating something, nothing

While a few floors down
The occupants throw stones
Onto the terrace,

Watch them fall
In antic thuds. Outside
A tire spins off its axle

Rolls and flops
Into a sluggish pond.
The driver swears

While anglers set their poles
And wait in steady rain,
Ignore the gypsies

Scouring trash heaps
Just beyond.
Night falls

And in another wing
A radio plays lovesongs
In Italian, French

As vodka bottles smash
Onto the flags,
And through the pond

Their webbed feet
Tangled in the algae,
Feathers stiff with mud

Eight ducks paddle
Struggle
Quacking to the beat.

Bathing

Gulliver with breasts,
I wedge myself
Into a Lilliputian tub
Struggle with outlandish spigots
Missing plugs
An alien stream
Of liquid
From an unknown source
A concrete cake of soap

And suddenly observe
Familiar shapes embossed on vinyl:
Stylized suns with curled coronas
Spaced predictably above
An argosy of Viking ships
Dragon figureheads and flags,
Symmetrical parade of sail
Through plastic waves, the motion
Orderly, almost majestic.

Then I see
They've hung the curtain sideways
And the graceful fleet
Drains slowly
Down the unplugged pipe.

Surveillance

(for Laura)

Those ominous babushkas sidling down
The hallways, knives jammed in their belts or clenched
In wrinkled fists, those semiautomatics
Stuffed in threadbare coats: guards see it all.

In every shabby highrise, on each floor
At every entrance, every gate, they watch.
Their eyes scan every movement, Cerberus
In tweed or Argus in a flannel shirt.

Clones of Zhivago in his later years
Down to the laser gaze and fraying cuffs
They wear red arm bands, kings of empty space
And dingy corridors, tired sovereigns

Of vacant desks and half-filled cups of tea
Barons of the radio and lords
Of ashtrays where they leave their cigarettes
A pungent wreath of smoke to mark their stay.

Middle-aged or more, their faces worn
But handsome, thoughts caged in the Terror, they
Pick up all and nothing to protect
Their ragged realms. They wait. They always wait

For masked intruders sneaking up the stairs
Or hiding just behind the peeling door,
For anarchists who bring *plastique*, those young
Assassins in high heels and skimpy skirts
Below sheer blouses, stalkers of the world.

Lenin's Tomb

We surrender
Everything
Before we can approach

The monolith in red and black
Porphyry and granite
Rising from the cobbles

In a permanent epiphany
While armed guards
Order silence, lead us

Down those darkened stairs
That flow like arteries
Straight from their heart

A glass sarcophagus
Encasing one small shape
Of history, one artifact,

Its edges sealed from everything
Waxy features fixed
Beneath their crystal coffin

Change arrested
Underneath the carefully directed
Light, bright center

In a labyrinth
Of dark, the tight face
Absolute, small cheekbones

Slanting toward the past
And future, East and West
Enfolding difference

Like the double-headed eagle
Of the Romanovs,
Their old imperial seal

More like them
Than he could have guessed
While people tiptoe by the shrine

And later speak
Of burying old icons
From his century

Which rests
Immobile
Underneath the probing light.

At the Museum of the Revolution

In dusty stacks beneath a table
Underneath large posters
Showing Marx and Engels, Lenin,
Workers of the world for sale
Suddenly I find Walt Whitman
Gazing up at me,
His robust features caught
On yellowed paper
Long beard thick, full-throated,
Sweeping off the page.
Perhaps he would have liked
These new-found comrades
Pledged to the encompassing
Of North and South, East and West
Containing all those multitudes
In endless lines
Of blowing bugles, beating drums
The present, future
Steppes, pine forests, seas
In life or death forever.

In another room
I see the paintings, records,
Rifles, cannon, clothing of the Revolution
Grave insignia of victories and May Day rites
Along with relics of the czars,
Their prisons, whips, and clubs.
I view photographs
Of serfs mired to their waists in mud
Guns aimed at the Romanovs
And then I wonder
How his own war days, those long nights
Spent with dying men in Washington
Those hours in septic surgeries
Might have colored

All the Russian elegies and catalogues
That Whitman never wrote,
Where he might have placed
The star, lilac, thrush
Measureless with love
In life or death forever.

Reds

In Russian
Words for *beautiful* and *red*
Curl around each other,
Root on root, like arms of lovers
Caught in a long embrace.

Red girls
With their crimson smiles
Walk arm in arm
Through rows of bursting apple trees
On August afternoons.

Red waves roll
At sunrise
Down glass walls
Into the Moscow River
Mirroring red domes.

Red carnations
Mark the places
Where old patriots
Sleep beautifully beneath
The cobbles on Red Square.

In country houses
Old Believers
Worship at the Red Corner
Icons stiff with reverence
Gold leaf, lace,

And in cathedrals
Red peels off
The robes of saints. Flecks
Of plaster fall
To waiting hands.

Pillars in red porphyry
Line Metro stops
Like armies,
Soldiers caught forever
In a red salute,

While firebirds
Stretch their blazing wings
Drop red feathers
On the pages
Of a thousand books.

Crimson currents run
Through Red October
Centuries before and after
Red stars spinning
On the Kremlin towers,

Revolutions
Throwing sparks
Into the lives
That pulse
Along red streets.

And even when the lights
Go off
Red marks ends
Beginnings
Absolute convergence

Of the blood's red melodies,
Words and rhythms
Faces, places
Fusion as complete
As love.

Amber

Coiled on my dresser
Like a watchful snake
The necklace glows
Still warm from wear

Almost alive
About to spring
Onto the nearest chair
Or table, glide

Toward the door,
A world of sun outside.
I can not picture
This collected heat

As hardened blood
Of old trees dying
On the Baltic
In a lost millennium

Stiffening through centuries
For eager hands
To gather,
Fragments of gold light

Strung into chains and bracelets
Giant combs
Facing for the bedroom
Of a Czar.

I see only
Imminent life
Drawing tight into its core
Waiting for the chance

To strike.

Rubles

They glitter in abandoned lots
Peer up from grass
Like spectral eyes
Fall from windows
To the pavement
In a brass cascade.

Double-headed eagles
By the tens of thousands
Wings trapped in tarnished rims
Bearings lost
They are worthless now
A waste of space in empty wallets

But we scramble for them,
Fight the way
We used to do
For Easter eggs
Or marbles
In the ring.

They shine
Like medals
On the threadbare coats
Of veterans who walk the dusty streets
Of Moscow or St. Pete,
Survivors of the Patriotic War.

They shine like crosses
Round the necks of thin babushkas
Who leave nothing
For the garbage man,
Breathe their last
In airless flats.

I watch for serendipities of light
In vacant tennis courts
Pretentious boulevards
Or tangled in the weeds
Around white birches in the park.
They shine.

Lacemaker

Not more than twenty-five,
Hair sagging on her neck
In limp festoons, her shirt
Torn at the sleeve,
She hunches over black rosettes
And curlicues,
Winds filaments of silk
Into a scalloped scarf
A midnight filigree
Designed
For some romantic evening
In a shark's Mercedes
While the train rocks
Back and forth
Between brief stops,
Swaying in the dark
From one illuminated station
To the next
Through dusty tunnels
Intersections tangled
Like a heap of ragged fringe,
Air thick as hemp.

Moscow Metro

Every ninety seconds
Trains roll into sumptuous stations,
Spaces gilded, fluted
Painted, carved

Pillars with Corinthian capitals
Mosaics nine feet wide
And in a dozen colors
Lenin's face on epic scale

Mythic workers of the world
Set in murals of the Revolution
Testaments
In high relief.

No plaque lists the names
Of those who framed
The black oak pediments
Or furrowed art

Into the columns
Chiseled idylls into marble
Dug the tunnels
Shored up sagging vaults.

No one counts
Those ghosts who vanished
Under rocks
Or in a freeze

Tiles laid up by men and women
Living on a lump of suet
Sometimes bread and sugar cubes
Each day

Masonry completed, dark tracks
Hammered into place
By writers, doctors, architects
Professors lost to law

Because they once forgot some ritual
Or wrapped their fish bones in a sheet
Of newsprint showing Stalin's face,
Men and women
In the millions
Broken by utopia.

Babushka's Monologue

I don't like the Metro, dark caves filled
With hurrying and noise, those moving stairs
That make me dizzy, but the steel cars rock
My body back and forth the way the wind
Once pushed me through tall grass outside Zagorsk
Where I grew up, the woods alive with bees
And small white butterflies, white birches high
As Nizhni's Kremlin, flowers everywhere.
I learned to use a scythe and work a plow
On days that stretched like crosses on the tops
Of domes. My father said that loving earth
Was all. But here it's dust all summer, grit
That settles in the creases of my face
And fingers, even lines my sleeves. I dream
Of cold that cleanses street and sky, sweeps all
Heat's leavings with its stiff white broom and soothes
The eyes. When snow comes, I make soup for young
Natasha, sheathe her in red scarves and coats
Each morning, bless her as she leaves for school.
She sleeps with me. I listen to her sounds,
Her quiet breathing, pull the blankets tight
To keep her warm. The older girl attends
Four classes at the University,
Wears perfume and short skirts, spends hours before
Our new machine that sews where she makes up
Sheer blouses like the ones you see in fine
Stores for the rich. Her hair shines in the sun.
She says my face is lined and rubs thick cream
Along my neck to make the wrinkles fade.
I laugh and keep my kerchief on. In our
Old days of Terror no one went to church
But now I go two times a week. I hear
The chants and smell the incense, pray to all
The saints who listen in their holy rooms
Although the noise here may drown out my words.

Maybe they do not know what happens hour
By hour in daylight, by the kiosks, streets
And stairs, so now I cross myself each time
I pass the holy gates, touch sainted walls
And think about these things while I am on
The train, its motion rocking me the way
I did my children once. Sometimes I still
Feel tall grass swirling, dancing at my knees.

Matriochkas

You see them everywhere
That tourists go,
Nesting dolls by hundreds
Lustrous red enamel and gold leaf
In layers
Over linden or white birch,
Women carrying Russia in their bellies
Mothers pregnant with the motherland
Forever
Symmetries of strawberries
And fairy tales
Forests, czars,
Scenes from Pushkin
Or the rural life
Painted carefully
Repeatedly
Across a rounded waist.

They smile eternally
Eyes luminous with expectation
Lashes curled and fanning out
Like a corona
Cheeks a perfect Russian red
Girl within girl
Woman in woman
Mother in mother
Womb in womb
Concentric mysteries
Each revealing and concealing,
Closing, opening
To show another
And another
Toward a core
No one can name, a cipher
Glowing red, blue, gold.

Underground Musicians

Beneath those killer streets
In grimy subways where we walk
Through corridors that lead
To crowded prospects
With their stalls
And vendors hawking trinkets
For the West

Rise the voices
Of a violin, accordion
Guitar and balalaika
Sax and trumpet
Somehow solitary
In the noise
Separate from everything

Except the melodies
Of Schubert
Bach and Mozart
Beatles and Bob Dylan
Folksongs from the steppes
Remote as ice floes
In the heat of passing flesh.

We stride along,
Throw rubles, dollars
Into hats or open cases
Colors of the currency
Lost in the wider spectrum
Of a baritone's crescendo
Or the flutist's final trill

Colored notes
With pictures of the Kremlin
Or George Washington

Irrelevant designs
That gather
In the dust and dark
While someone finishes a waltz.

Paul Robeson in Russia

He looks down that lonesome road
And steals away,
Leaves Jim Crow standing
On the Mississippi banks
To find another river
In his veins
Another trumpet sounding in his soul.

He works with the boatmen
Pulls the rope with them
Their anguish in his long embrace
Songs throbbing in his linebacker's chest
Rolling from his throat
In Volga blues

Before the chariot swings low
And carries him
Above the steppes,
Birches in white litanies
All the way to Moscow.
Applause before, behind him

He builds melodies
Above the wars
That fume in gated *dachas*
Secret spaces in the Kremlin
Hidden laboratories
Even in the camps.

Majestic in his slightly crinkled smile
His broken nose
He sings in the streets
To one, to all
Before he travels on,
Searching out the ways
To Jordan.

At the Tretyakov Gallery, Moscow

Its lemon-tinted rooms hold objects made
For dreams no one escapes: grand dukes and czars
Exalted, brutalized in marble, bars
And epaulettes like claws. Their contours fade
To icy slush as three young orphans, paid
In kopecks, drag a troika stuffed with jars
Of water up a hill against faint stars,
Frail human livestock in thin coats. But jade
And rubies round her neck, across the hall
A plump pink countess smoothes her satin gown,
Expecting some new beau. She combs her hair
And poses for her portrait, unaware
Of all the warnings, her days soon to drown
In flame and blood, Rasputin on the wall.

Cathedral of the Dormition, Zagorsk

Saints are everywhere.
White swallows fly above their heads
In perfect circles

Halos fluttering all day
Around the star-encrusted domes.
Inside, large eyes of the holy

Shine through centuries
Of peeling plaster, fading paint
Gold leaf pocked by rifle butts

Carved doors closed for decades.
Luminous gazes see it all:
Tatars, Poles, and Stalin

Sieges broken
In a canticle of flame
A litany of guns.

Now young women
Hunch above their sickly children,
Old ones lost in melody

And men line up to touch
The empty coffin of St. Sergius,
His bones caressed to dissolution

While they hear the choirs of baritones
Voices throbbing in the vaults.
Chants flow like holy water

Gathered in old bottles
Radiating through the dark with incense
And the heavy air of faith.

Old Believers limp
Toward benediction falling
Like a shaft of light

Dropped from the highest point
Of the highest dome,
Gold motes streaming down

Forever on their heads,
Sun following their weary feet
Into the spangled afternoon.

At the Nizhny-Novgorod Depot

Dusk is falling in the railyard.
Scattered lights
Begin to glitter
On the hills.
We drag our luggage
Through the rubble
Piles of rocks
Between the kiosks
Oily puddles from the rain
Grimy residue
Of one day's life:
Orange and banana peels
Broken bottles
Paper, cigarettes
Drunks passed out
Between the potholes.

We have almost reached our track
The waiting sleeper train
That runs to Moscow
When a boombox suddenly erupts
And music throbs into the night
Voices aching for the homeland,
Summer, lost love or a sentimental street
With an unintelligible name.
Now vagrants leave their corners,
Start to dance, join the choruses
Bare feet trying out the steps
Dodging trash and urine
Leaving just for now
Their broken world
And dancing, singing
In the failing light.

Proposition

Finishing a beer on the veranda,
Taking in the Volga
Counting hydrofoils
Their engines throbbing quietly
Along the turbid stream

I hear a husky voice
Behind me
Turn to see
A vast shirt
Blazing with Hawaiian scenes
Hibiscus by the score
Gold chains dripping
On a thickened neck
Pager bulging at his belt
Fillings glittering
Behind his smile
Like sunset on Oahu,
Dawn at Diamond Head.

I feel his sultry urgency
In words I haven't learned
But tones I know.
I tell him
I don't know his tongue.
He doesn't care.
He's dreaming of the West,
Czar Peter loaded down
To triviality and lust
A heated pool
His own Trans Am.

Icon of the moment,
I refuse
This fleeting canonization

My guest appearance with Don Ho
And turn back toward my room,
Grass skirts rustling faintly
In my wake.

Raising the Drawbridge, St. Petersburg

We gather
After midnight
For our offbeat pilgrimage
Walk quietly
Into the blueblack world outside,

Line up by the Neva
Watch life pour
Along the bridge
In crowded taxis, urgent trucks
As warning lights begin to flash.

A few cars
Race across the apex
On a dare, engines high,
Tires squealing, final moments
Traced in shrieks and laughter

Throbbing stereos.
At first the sections
Seem to stay in place
But then
They part,

A Roman arch
Stretched slowly into Gothic
Split finally to separate lines
Almost parallel, two vague monoliths
Floating on black waves,

Their weight and mass exalted
By the hidden gears and secret workings
Levers moving somewhere in the night,
Dark rising
Into something darker.

Fire-Gilding St. Isaac's

This dome,
Third largest in Eurasia
Dazzles trees, sky, even the sun.

Our guide explains "galvanoplasty":
Application of an alloy formed of gold
And mercury, shimmering liquid
Brushed on solid surfaces
Then set to flame.
The mercury burns off,
Gold now bonded to its base.

We also learn
About the sixty quitrent serfs,
Bonded slaves
Who burned off too
Their fevers rising in a sheen
To make this dome
Blaze in the mist

Its poison necessary
And inevitable
To create a perfect circle
Ring of God
More gold
Than Jordan, Troy
Even the Promised Land.

Tourists look straight up,
Their whispers rising
In a vapor toward the top.

At Peterhof

I wander with five hundred
Other tourists
Through this playground of the czars,
Stroll through formal gardens
Hedges trimmed to filigree
Orchestrated water
Flowing on large tiles
Below a gold leaf god
Water leaping to the heavens
Brilliant blues and greens
In iridescent arcs
Along the Gulf of Finland.

But further down
I find trick fountains,
Peter's sense of humor
Waiting for the fawning courtier,
The sycophant who takes one step
Too many
Or too few
And feels a jet of freezing water
Spouting toward his nose
Or periwig or crotch,
The leader's antic legacies outliving
Every solemn document he wrote.

Dancers and musicians dressed like Mozart
Carry off the velvet waistcoats
Breeches, frills. One of them
Asks me to join him in the promenade
And suddenly
I'm lifted into taffeta and silk,
My bodice jeweled with pearls
My feet uncovering
The delicate tracery of minuets,

Lost elegance in buckled shoes
A stately progress
While the court looks on, agape.

The music ends.
He bends before my hand,
Looks up, and whispers
"That will be three dollars, please."
Now I feel
Cold water shooting up my leg.

Street Symphony

Melodies begin
At midnight
When the crew arrives
To haul away the trolley
And repair the track
Outside my window,
Curses and jackhammers
Rising through the dark
In a furious duet.

Morning brings
A shrill aubade
Of diesels whining over bridges
In their acrid caravans.
Trams clatter through our breakfast
Ragged fanfares
In our kasha
And arpeggios of squeaking doors
Drop in our tea.

Later, we bang pavement
Watch guards start a fugue
With housemaids
Followed by a screaming voluntary
While babushkas groan
At the price of everything
And a motley band
Blares "Dixie" for the Alabama tourists
As their sleek bus rolls away.

Finally, at twilight
When we want to blow up everything
Some nun or monk, invisible
Inside the battered walls,
Begins to ring the bells for vespers
And we stop
Arrested

86

Fuses in our hands
To hear the changes
Old hymns
Glowing in the night.

The Virgin of Vladimir

Our guide
Describes the icons in detail:
Application of gold leaf on linden
Pigments blended
Into red
And otherworldly blue
Shapes stretched to holiness.

Suddenly I feel
The presence
Of a woman's gaze.
I find her
Set in glass
Gold-flecked,
A single panel
In a single room.

Her eyes command me
Keep me watching
While she thinks about her baby
Lost completely
In his bright new life,
No interest in the visitors
Who shuffle through her world.

She knows,
Accepts already
Just how brief his time will be.
Already he's a man,
His head almost as large
His arms as long
As those that cradle him.

He too sees
How little time there is

To touch, to look
To think of anything
Except his pitiless ascent,
Knowledge flat and unambiguous
As her red robe.

He reaches toward his mother,
Puts one arm around her neck.
His perfect fingers stroke her face
As for a while
He seeks
And finds
Protection from Gethsemane.

On the Eve of Departure

Heat rises with red wine and laughter
In the crowded Georgian restaurant
Where we gather
One last time.

Chairs, hands, and fingers
Tangle as we reach for course on course:
Spiced salads, cabbage soup, a tray
Of meats and cheese bread,
Champagne and vodka
For the wordy Russian toasts.

I look
Through grimy windows
Toward a courtyard
And a single hawthorne
Anchoring an empty swing.

Conservatory students
Dressed like gypsies
In black satin
Serenade us
Entertain us
Music studded with a thousand rhinestones

Catching, throwing light
With every movement of their hands,
Each strum and stroke
Guitar and balalaika,
Longing and leave-taking
Set in shimmering glissandi
Fevered rhapsodies and minor chords.
One throaty baritone recalls:

"Those were the days, my friend,

we thought they'd never end..."

We follow the musicians
Through the courtyard
And our last white night
Through labyrinths
Of white birch and gold domes
Rising like refrains in that half light

Until we reach the red stars
Of the Kremlin, colors dropping
From the towers like grace-notes
In the river just below,
While step by step
We start to move away.

IV. A Web of Green: Home

Redbuds

They start in February
Hard knots
On gray branches

Growing slowly
In the rain and cold
Like dreams remembered
Bit by bit
Until one morning

They erupt
In miles of lavender lace
Festoon the streets
With unexpected color, lavish life
Like someone singing Verdi in a parking lot

Before they vanish
In a web
Of green.

April in Pharr

(for Patty and Helmut)

Wind lifts the land:
Sunflowers take off
In all directions
Bougainvilleas ascending from trashcans
Palm fronds rattling above dusty streets.
The neighbor's moonbounce
Tugs at its moorings.
Even the noontime siren
Floats up in an endless spiral.

Everything starts to fly:
Raptures of chacalacas
Aubades of whippoorwills
Parliaments of jays and green parrots
Golden-throated woodpeckers and kiskadees
Chirping on telephone wires
In grapefruit and olive trees
As they start the pilgrimage.

In the end, we all grow wings,
Sprout bedraggled feathers
Just enough to lumber east
Toward the Gulf
Flapping awkwardly
Above the fields of levitating cabbages
Heading slowly toward a weighty world
Of clumsy pelicans
And punk-rock gulls.

Hailstorm

They said
It would move fast
But we were not prepared

For lightning splitting morning
Like a whiplash
Street lamps burning

Through the breakfast hour.
Nor could we take in
All the icy dancers

Bouncing on the parched St. Augustine
In their hysterical ballet,
Hoofers in and out of step

Entropic leaps
Like popcorn
Chaotic chorus lines

Performing random pirouettes,
The work
Of crazed apprentices

Hiding somewhere
In the sky, lost
In their magic words.

Finally released, the corps
Stretched out on driveways, flower beds
Sagging oaks

Throwing off
Their limp white costumes
Slowly flattening

Beneath a soggy sun
While we debated
Where

To begin
The day.

Summer Sky

Clouds sprawl across late afternoon
Like a harem,
Nudes billowing
In strawberry cream
And languishing toward dusk,
Luminous shapes
That Rubens might have heaped
Onto his canvas every night,
Gently pushing
Those voluptuous arms
Into position
Folding fingers
Just behind the neck
Taking a moment
To arrange the strands
Of red gold hair
Before he found his brush
And painted them
Into the heavens,
Streaking light across the evening,
Dripping colors on the floor.

In the Garden

Dirt caked beneath my fingernails
Sweat rolling down my face
I set in salvia
Red yarrow and petunias
Fighting slugs and pillbugs
For each bloom
My knees on fire
While freckles
In their speckled armies
March across my back.

Heat builds.
I start to think of other gardens,
First my neighbors' plots
And then that first one
All green velvet, ecstasy in bloom
Eve in her perfect world
Eve with her pearly arms
No sweat, rain only on demand
No toil or aching muscles
Insects in proportion.

Resentment grows
Like Johnson grass
And dandelion.
I never ate that apple
Never gulled a helpless male
But still I pay for hybris
Aspiration gone astray
Or is it fallen hormones
DNA run wild
A midlife crisis?

The sun has climbed too nigh
For speculation.

I go indoors
To post-Lapsarian air conditioning
But watch the contests
Raging through my windows
Hibiscus taking on the ants
And struggling up on leathery stalks
To sound a blood-red trumpet
Proclaiming gritty miracles.

A Night on Padre Island

Flat on my back, sand wedged
Between my teeth, fogging my ears
Sandcrabs burrowing around my toes
I thought I would grow into the beach
Root a stand of ghost-gray sunflowers.
I would become a dune, Lot's wife
In another place.

Instead I gazed
Straight up
Into a storm of light.
The sky rained stars that night
Constellations pouring on my head.
The Little Dipper ladled blue and yellow
Through the dark
Drenched my gritty quilt.

I woke next morning
To a perfect calm
The sun well up
But still felt stars
Their burning edges
Everywhere.

Vegetable Love in Texas
(for Dick)

Farmers say
There are two things
Money can't buy:
Love and homegrown tomatoes.

I pick them carefully.
They glow in my hands, shimmer
Beneath their patina of warm dust
Like talismans.

Perhaps they are.
Summer here is a crucible
That melts us down
Each day,

The sky a sheet of metal
Baking cars, houses, streets.
Out in the country
Water-starved maize

Shrivels into artifacts
A desiccated cache
Of shredded life.
Farmers study archeology

In limp straw hats.
But still I have
This feeble harvest
Serendipity in red

Red like a favorite dress
Warm like a dance
Lush like a kiss long desired,
Firm like a vow, the hope of rain.

August

In desert cities
We seek dark, those spaces
Without sun
Find salvation
In a single spindly mesquite
Porches with the deepest overhang
Porticoes that shut out everything
But breeze
The dankness of a stone arcade
Anything to heal the heat.

For here
Light is extinction:
A grove of charcoal trees, the sky
A line of fire, grass cross-hatched
In tones of gray and brown
Like someone's woodcut of the Final Judgment
Dug into the landscape
With a molten plow
Heaven ending everything each day
Except the memory
Of green.

Tracking Hurricane Ike
(for Emily)

Newsmen air footage nonstop:
Rising water battering the Seawall,
Wind bending palms
Into parabolas,
Half of Houston
Submerged.

But I am thinking of another sea,
Another time
When my teenaged grandchild
Pulled me into the waves.
Then the photo: spray rising around us
In an iridescent bubble
Above white-sugar sand
And turquoise swells,
Her long arms wrapped around my waist
Her hair a golden storm
Something Botticelli might have brushed
One sunny afternoon.

For that instant
We are safe in the eye-wall
Of each other's arms,
Sheltered for the moment
From all the tempests waiting,
Hard squalls that will come
The next day or the next
In emails and text messages,
Offices and classrooms
Courtrooms and bedrooms,
Rising water everywhere.
I hold her tight.

Lunar Eclipse

The weathermen agreed
We would not see another one
This century.

I waited in the driveway,
Watched
The cold familiar cup

Fill mile by mile
With distant wine,
Some tint

I'd never seen before
Closest to a dusky rose
Poured

By invisible fingers
Gripping
A transparent flask

The whole thing staged
In an ordinary sky
On an ordinary night.

No dogs
Barked in frenzy. No cats
Yowled at demons.

No villagers
Beat gongs, pots, pans
To drive the shade away

No werewolves, vampires, bats
Just light
Elusive light

Unnamed color
Flowing into everything
Moving silently

And slowly vanishing,
Leaving us
In luminous dust.

Another Ode to Autumn

This isn't Keats:
Dew smudges windshields
Leaves clutter sidewalks
Acorns plop and clatter on pavement
Beneath parliaments of fowl
Chattering in hackberries.
Grackles strut, squawk on grass
In blue-black gaggles,
Querulous majorettes in mourning.
Clumsy pyramids of pumpkins
Monopolize parking lots
While a buzzard wheels ominously
Around a neighbor's back yard.

Yet this time has its offbeat majesty:
Morning mist spirals off a field
In luminous plumes. A sapphire noon
Dazzles everything. Leaves float by
In their weightless waltz
Silence of afternoon
Broken now and then
By the dropping of a late-blooming rose
Or a sudden swirl of wings.
At dusk a firefly glides along the street,
Lighting our lawns in sporadic bursts
Before Orion starts to glitter
And a new moon curls above the horizon
Like a sleeping child.

Galveston in October

The sea is German silver here,
A molten mass that never cools
Heavy metal singing
In a cauldron. Nothing ever stops.

A hundred palms along the Seawall
Dance like Fred Astaire and Ginger Rogers
Green fronds waltzing cheek-to-cheek
Against a backdrop of gray silk.

Choruses of sea-oats
Beach plum, kelp
Roll in, roll out
All day, all night

And by the bay a square-rigged barque
Sways at her pier, masthead tilting
In the wind like some lost woman
Looking for a permanent address.

Sand shifts each second, drifts through thoughts
And pastel rooms. Even antebellum dowagers
Rock slowly with the waves, outlasting war
And storms, columns elegant, secure.

Nothing drowns this point and counterpoint
Bubbling in old pewter
Churning toward those closing chords
The ocean never plays.

Halloween on Sixth Street, Austin

An Angel in a loincloth
Bumps and grinds
Beneath the spotlight
Fluffy wings slowly swaying
As he writhes,
His body glistening.

Behind him two pianists
Bang out
"Give Me that Old-time Rock- n-Roll"
Toss down Shiner Bocks
Between the numbers
Their smooth arms shining
In the track lights.

Celebrating life and death
Two pirates
And a girl
Sheathed in pink saran
Dance belly to belly
While the Phantom of the Opera
And a human crocodile look on.

Behind the bar
A young Grim Reaper
Walks across the stage
On stilts
Cardboard scythe in his hand
Swinging toward the man
In a blue tutu.

Borders meet tonight
As thousands promenade
Between the barricades
And Generation Xers drift

Through the Middle Ages
Stumbling
In their academic robes.

Rock from one bar
Penetrates the rap of another
Like the gyres of Yeats
As men become women, women become panthers
Old become young
And time becomes elastic
For a night.

Texas Two-Step

Step 1: A night alive with stars
The Interstate strung with lights
Of passing cars
Strains of a Christmas concert
Still drifting through our ears.
We speed through dark
Taking in the sky
In eager breaths
Seeing now and then
Reminders of the road,
Universal symbols
In their yellow diamonds--
Dump trucks
On impossible inclines
Or falling rocks
Perhaps a deer
Freeze-framed
In a balletic leap.

Step 2: A fast-moving shadow
On the driver's side
Materializes in a twelve-point buck
Suddenly flopping on the hood
In shuddering thuds
Like some titanic trout
Reeled onto the deck of a passing ship.
His rack clatters on the windshield
A set of giant castanets
The grille contracting like an accordion
Before he crumples underneath the wheels.
We make it to the shoulder
Leap away from the smoke
Stumble along the roadside
Like drunks in a deserted dance hall
Waiting in the freezing dark
While stars blaze light to us
But not in time.

Advent

I hear no angel's trumpet
In the rattle of dry leaves along the street.
I see no luminous wings, no beatific gaze
Concealed in naked trees.

The sky does not remind me
Of stained glass. No stars burn down
Toward anything
But centuries of empty space.

I search but see
No pageant in the stores,
Just lines of weary men and women
Waiting to check out.

Their carts bulge underneath
White streamers drooping like bandages
Above the aisles. Large red snowflakes
Hang like meat from ceilings.

In the parking lot, someone
Is selling trees, strings of bulbs
Wrapped tight around the stumps,
A tourniquet, a clamp.

But I am looking for some other tree.
I wait to hear some scratching at the screen
A key explode a rusty lock,
Perhaps a puny wail
In rocks and twisted roots
To write new history everywhere.

New Year's Eve, San Antonio
(for Emilie)

Just before midnight
And the new year's rowdy birth
We stumble into the street
Champagne glasses in our hands
To herald the delivery.

We start to sing
An off-key "Auld Lang Syne"
And a neighbor breaks the law,
Sets off Roman candles
In his yard.

Suddenly night explodes
In temporary stars. Small galaxies
Of red, green, gold, they spin over roofs
And treetops, spiral down toward grass
And gravel, vanish finally in frost.

But in that time
Light fills our chilly space.
Our voices float
Through darkness,
Rise above it.

We too become stars,
Tipsy avatars
Shining in brief counterpoint
To everything
The old year brought.

Writer's Block in the Old South

Poems used to gallop to my door
Earnest messengers of love, death, war
Lathered horses huffing in the heat.
Words waltzed merrily across the page
Running the blockade of work and time,
Rhett Butler whirling Scarlett
Through Virginia reels
Swinging her weightlessly
Into the dance.

Today poems dawdle on the outskirts of my mind
Like Prissy counting fenceposts
On her way back from the doctor.
She plays with her apron, hums her songs
While Melanie moans in labor
And Yankees batter Georgia
Wounded Rebels lying in dusty rows
Around the depot
Just before Atlanta falls.

I need a lyric crisis,
Some obsessive mission
That would galvanize my lazy muse,
A frantic exit
Through a burning city
One furious kiss
New vows made
Against a sprawling sunset
Huge rays lighting everything.

Lines Composed in the Computer Classroom

We're studying discs tonight.
Like Adam made anew
I wander through the cyber garden
Paradise of facts
Naming files, opening and closing them
Eating their strange fruit.

But soon I fall.
Seduced by thoughts of sleep
I drift
And suddenly
I'm in a wilderness of icons
Where the files can't go.

I stumble on the Internet
And open "Tennyson."
At first I am regaled
By subtle arguments
On the Laureate's long life
His friendships, labored love.

Then by accident
(Or is it serpents in the monitor?)
The loss of Hallam seems too much.
I hit something
And a hundred Dow-Jones quotes
Explode onto the screen.

It's too late
For fortunes to be made and lost.
I seize the mouse
And click "escape"
Thinking of the garden just outside
Redolent of pine, thick with silent stars.

Looking at a Painting by Rousseau

(for Connor)

The forest pulls me in:
Hypnotic trees
Mythic green
A shade unknown anywhere else
Those fairy-tale leaves.

I walk beside sleepy cows
Too contented to graze.
Milkmaids wander drowsily
Through silent groves.
They too are spellbound,
Leaving their chores undone
Unhampered by their heavy gowns.

I want to curl into this idyll
Nod off somewhere in the dream
My head against an otherworldly oak
Like Rip Van Winkle
Missing decades of the evening news,
Sleeping through reports of bullets flying
Blood and hunger everywhere

Before the guard
Comes by
To shake my shoulder
Hustling me
Into another room.

Itzhak Perlman Concert

He clanked onstage
In lurching metal arcs
Legs forced into his tux,
Braces dragging
On the polished floor.

He sat
At last,
Took the violin
From his accompanist
As if it were a sleeping child

And suddenly
We flew,
Blue air
Sharp
As ice

Saw rainforests
In their deep demonic green,
Interiors of orchids
Dangling from their giant trees
Like ghosts.

We raced through rain
In Paris,
Listened to Beethoven
Pound heroic measures
While he still could hear.

We were not ready
For the silence,
Never satisfied
And so
We stood

Alive
To nothing
But this hour
Shining
Through the darkened space.

Dress Rehearsal, *Tosca*
(for Catherine)

It's slightly off at first:
The diva overweight
A French horn flat
Random noise offstage
An irascible conductor
Shouting at the harpist
Puccini's luscious arias
Broken into jagged chunks.

Then sound lifts me
Into the story:
Evil forthright in black velvet
And white lace
Lust dripping down a wine glass
Intrigue unfolding everywhere
The soprano's love sheared
To notes beyond the register.

Her songs leap chasms,
Scale the years
And suddenly a man I loved
When I was twenty
Walks onstage.
Still young, he pours out
Our time in soaring melodies
Decades vanished in a breath.

After all the blood and knives
Poisons real and imagined
Melodrama and puny plots
We sing our dreams
Beneath the stars, above sweet-smelling earth
Never loving life so much as now
In a darkened auditorium
Watching dawn spread over Rome.

Mozart Making Bread

Baking for my children
I put on *The Magic Flute*
And suddenly
He's in the kitchen

Pots and pans
Horns and violas
Piled high around him
Lumps of batter on the floor.

Hands caked with flour
Humming strains from some new opera
He braids melodies into the dough
Manufactures intrigue in the oven

While he kneads and pounds
His hold-out diva
Bars of a yeasty aria
Taking shape between his fingers.

Never mind the deadlines
Scalding creditors
Salzburg's drafty rooms
The Emperor's dismissal.

He rests a moment
Dreams of other works
Before things heat up again
And his balky lover

Sings at last
Bubbles to a crescendo
Warm and fragrant
In my hands.

Ballade of the *Nutcracker* Matinee
(for Emily)

My grandchild wriggles in her seat and whines
For candy bars until the trumpets bore
Into the theater. A spotlight shines
And curtains rise as dancers take the floor
To spin into the famous story, pore
Over their gifts, and dream. No longer tired,
She quickly learns good timing, narrow door,
That line between the real and the aspired.

This afternoon it's perfect. Clara finds
Her Prince. They oust the Mouse King and restore
The Sugar Plums. She pirouettes twelve times,
Twirls ecstatically. And when they soar
Into the *pas de deux*, that magic core
Of Clara's night, the cast looks on, beguiled
As he catches her midair, ends the war,
That line between the real and the aspired.

Years hence, when they have aged and each joint grinds
Legs thickened like old gravy, life a chore
The Prince's hands reduced to nervous vines
When my grandchild ponders the murky lore
Of Tchaikovsky's depression, ghosts that roar
On every page of script, his genius mired
In doubt and darkness, she'll love all the more
That line between the real and the aspired

Recalling a December day that tore
Through time, a day when we were weightless, wired
To float onstage, our toes poised to explore
That line between the real and the aspired.

On *The Shawshank Redemption*

The prison operates
Like Janus in razor wire
Twin profiles facing opposite directions.
One face looks out on suffering.
It rises like a Juggernaut
In dark gray rows, tightly seamed
Like one of Shawshank's walls:
Worm-riddled grits
Phallic nightsticks swinging through the years
Like dislocated pendulums
Months in the hole
Bull queers checking out the field
The warden's unctuous smile
Claudius in a pinstriped suit.

The other face:
Brooks with a bird in his pocket
Inmates guzzling beer on a rooftop
Or gazing toward heaven
As Mozart floats
Through the p.a. system
While Andy tunnels to freedom with a rock hammer
Crawls through the underworld
Emerging on the other side baptized
His stolen suit pristine
After his trip through the sewer
Transportation to the banks
Somehow arranged
The warden's scams laid open like a boil.

And yet I believe it all, believe
That Red will play his new harmonica.
Brooks will find Jake
And Tommy won't be killed.
I follow Andy to the open road.

I am with him in his red convertible
Wind whistling in my hair.
We drive down to Mexico
Lean into the hairpin turns
That lead to the Pacific,
Ocean with no memory
Nothing but a sapphire crescent
Cradling white sand, bare feet,
A shining face.

Portrait of a Guitarist: A Rondeau
(for Liz)

Bent into flamenco, he plays nonstop
Pressing out the chords like wine, drop by drop,
Above her piano. Ten years ago
She saw him in a gallery, the glow
Of his eyes, lashes thick as frets, that mop

Of charcoal hair. She brought him home. He hopped
From serenade to ballad, sowed a crop
Of melodies that made dark roses grow
Bent into flamenco,

Or a sonata bright with a dollop
Of strums. Sometimes she had to leave her shop
To hear those sounds, and then his hands would flow
Across the room to touch her face or throw
A kiss before he took it from the top,
Bent into flamenco.

Multi-tasking

My daughter—
Talking on her cell
Reading mail
Paying bills
Watching *Oprah*—
Says I need to multi-task
Or I'll be left behind.
I balk and then remember:

Grandmother would crochet
Her scores of sweaters
Colors falling to her feet
In heaps of red, pink, blue, green
A scattered rainbow on the floor
Eccentric snowflakes in July
While she watched Raymond Burr
As Perry Mason.

He too was good at multiple operations,
Dazzling the viewers
With his smoldering eyes
Languidly answering the phone
In the middle of a crisis
Directing Della to her typewriter
Or Paul to his endless errands
Before entering the courtroom

To mete out Burger's weekly loss
The prosecution doomed from the start
With "incompetent, irrelevant, and immaterial,"
Mason's mantra for all occasions.
Grandmother would take it in
While she finished a shawl,
Mopped floors or peeled a carrot.
Grandfather would rib her

For her failure to identify the murderer.
She could have solved the case
If she had dropped her mop or needle
For a while,
But she would turn to him
And stroke his cheek
Just as the killer was confessing.
Then they multi-tasked together.

Italian Restaurant in South Texas

Luigi takes us to his private dining room
Heaps tortellini and crepes florentine
On spotless plates. We eat politely,
Use the proper forks.
A young man enters, gives us cards:
"Alfredo Pauli, Massage Therapist."

He offers us a demonstration,
One full minute of massage
Starting with our hostess
Who is reaching for her wine.
I watch her face go blank,
Turn featureless like some large mollusk
While his fingers find the nerves
Along her shoulders
And her fork sits idle in her pesto

Like a rake left out to rust
In some large haystack,
Its faithless owner bingeing on a holiday
A Grant Wood reject
Missing out on the immortal pose.
Conversation dangles over cold linguini
As Alfredo comes to each of us in turn.
My spoon drifts aimlessly in marinara sauce,
My knife lost in a crepe.

We seem to pay the bill and amble toward the car
But really we are off in Venice
On our backs in some large gondola
Floating down the Grand Canal
Our fingers trailing in warm water
While we pass beneath the Bridge of Sighs.

A Flight to Lubbock

We make our final approach
And I prepare for boredom
Look out the window and see sky
Nothing but sky
An inverted blue ocean
Washing over fast-food signs and billboards
Red clay and corn fields
All flat and predictable as a grocery list
Until surprise geometry arcs before me
Irrigation lines in vast concentric circles
Stonehenge in the middle of the Llano Estacado.

Then the night:
A peacock iridescent as some headliner in Las Vegas
Lets me stroke his crown.
I gaze up at cobalt heavens
Glittering like something Elvis would wear
And see a showgirl of a moon.
She dances through thin clouds
Briefly wearing them like cosmic boas.

Mars grows closer, brighter somehow
Breaking the horizon light-years away
Bigger out here.
A street light shines
On an immigrant white maple
That should be in Vermont
Spinning its thousands
Of two-tone leaves, almost psychedelic
A reminder to keep my eyes open
Wide open
All the time.

Palo Duro Canyon

The magic show begins
A few miles out of town,
Makes high plains vanish
In thin air, pulls scarves
From sandstone hats
For twenty million years.
Gold and russet roar, red churns
On stones, blue hums in cottonwoods.
I never meet the conjurer
With all those colors up his sleeve
The sorcerer with boulders
In his hands, levitating caprock
Balancing an outcrop on his head.

I never hear his incantations
Dream instead of shades,
Almost see Georgia O'Keeffe
Scrambling up a hill, sketchbook
In her arms to paint some sensual poppy
All those epic flowers
Everything in motion swaying
Past the names designed
To keep them still: Sad Monkey, Goodnight,
Lighthouse, Prairie Dog Town.
I see it all, believe,
Before the artist finally escapes
Leaving just the props.

One Night in a Cheap Motel

Here, J. Alfred Prufrock
Might have started over,
Where flocks of pudgy pigeons
Waddle toward the dumpster
In a steady progress
And evening spreads its streams
Of red and gold
Across a half-deserted parking lot.

Inside, my feet stick
To gummy carpet. Freight trains pass
Through the room each hour,
The fury of their whistles
Shaking the faded print of Sorrento
Above my bed, and missile beer cans
Hurtle through open windows,
Disturb the universe.

No one here is etherized.
A tomcat sits by my door, courting me
In plaintive yowls. Doors lock and unlock
All night long, and through the walls
I hear disembodied laughter, sultry tones
Set to raucous country-western songs.
In the room above, people come and go
Probably not talking of Michelangelo.

The sun rises
On legions of bottles
Upright on window sills
Or sprouting in the grass
Like amber weeds, while oil-field workers
And their eager families,
Already smelling of the sea,
Load buckets, toys and towels
In their pickups for a day at the beach.
I almost hear the mermaids sing.

Town Homes in Houston

The Middle Ages are returning here:
Glass towers and granite griffins
Swimming pools behind pink palisades
And battlements guarded
By electric knights in cruisers
At the gated access
Monitoring moats
Around high walls.

Oleanders, jasmine, and hibiscus
Bloom in tropical pageantry,
Almost hide the wires
Behind the windows.
Ladies look out
From loopholes.
Intercoms guide yard men on the sidewalks,
Motion detectors and panic buttons everywhere.

What's missing is the allegory:
Journeys through the concrete forest
Queens out to watch a joust at Galleria,
Scholastics counting angels at the bank
Martyrs dying for their creeds in country clubs
While gaunt troubadours strum their lutes
And wander through the bayous,
Singing of lost love.

Refinery

The vast Miltonic landscape fills the night
Erupting through dark swamp land all the way
From Houston to Beaumont, a maze of pipes
And conduits twisted into towers, vats,
Deep tanks, surreal formations. Dante would
Have recognized these skylines of the damned
These watch lights by the hundreds studding dark,
A sterile copulation. Smokestacks come
In fetid bursts, white hot against the pines
Their vapor smothering the stars as rank
And file move past the fluid boundaries
Expanding Lucifer's preserve to stage
A hellish gala day and night, around
The clock, black crude transformed to shimmering
Convenience, incorporating sky
Warm seas of profitable alchemy
While trees turn gray, drop needles, leaves and limbs
All the way from Houston to Beaumont.

Jogging in New England

The Pilgrims hated all this sunless green
Those mosses inching up along the paths—
Ajuga, aspidistra, river fern

In ominous clumps beneath the drooping firs
Raindrops shimmering on tips of leaves
About to fall like Adam in his fragile

Paradise while stones erupted at
His feet in huge aberrant teeth. They caught
The jagged smell of pines and salty soil

With evil vapors rising in the night
To veil those others, muffling their words
And predatory steps, their dark removes.

I trot along those endless, winding roads
Remember William Bradford's fevered lines
About a dreadful wilderness, the lack

Of taverns in the woods, those natural men
Who hid behind the trees. Today it seems
Innocuous. A summer visitor,

I take in miles of green, feel slightly high
On salt marsh scent. But soon I fail to read
A sign and lose the way, pick up thick noise

Along the Interstate, a moaning rush
Of eighteen wheelers rolling into Boston
In ungainly covens carrying

Their unregenerate freight. I smell their rank
Exhaust as vapors fill the woods and drift
Toward clouds and tops of trees in acid plumes.

Suddenly I understand those words
Penned in the night by frantic, hungry saints,
Their desperate prayers gasped in a dark green world
For grace to find their solitary way.

Song for New Orleans

(to the victims of Hurricane Katrina)

Walt Whitman would love you
Even more today,
Grimy jewel of the South
Glowing in the foil
Of Big Muddy.
He would walk all over you,
Count the red brick buildings
Rich with soot
Streets bright with the heavy confetti
Of shopping bags and flyers.

He would amble through the French Quarter
Paint peeling from its facades
Its telephone wires sheathed in vines
Before he wolfed down gumbo in big bowls
Crab claws floating on top like mermaids
Everpresent as flashing breasts.
He would swallow Louie Armstrong's highest notes,
Gulp down jazz, blues, and zydeco
Breathe in the ghosts of Williams and Capote

Before he strolled Canal Street
Standing on the neutral ground
To take in multitudes:
The young man rapping on a corner
A harried intern racing to the hospital
Handcuffed teens
Piling out of the police van
Like reluctant clowns.
Maybe he would see the live show at Loew's
with the Voodoo Sex Queens from Outer Space.

Further out, beyond the Superdome, he would hear
The Natchez Queen puffing up the river
Like an athlete out of shape,
Or hitch a ride on the fabled train

Chugging through the heavy evening air,
Rich dark laughter
Shining like gold in an alley.
He would smell the sea and Lake Ponchartrain
Perfume and sweat, chicory, trash, and magnolias,
Catalogue the whorls on an oyster shell.

Later he might loaf along the levees
Stroke their voluptuous shoulders
Take his ease under oaks and sleepy cypresses
Spanish moss trailing from their limbs
Like tattered shawls.
He would pass
Through both the shotgun shacks
And antebellum dowagers of the Garden District
Becoming part of them,
Of everything.

Then, under a starry night
He would watch the endless pageants
Of streaming lights
To find his way to Duncan Plaza
Where Avery Alexander points the way
Leaning into civil rights
Remembering the auction block
Where John McDonough wants to do
"Good, much good, great good"
For his fellow man.

At last Walt would stretch out
By the homeless man
Asleep at the feet of George Washington
And dream,
Curled into the heart
Of New Orleans
Grimy jewel of the South
Glowing
In the foil
Of Big Muddy.

Titanic Exhibit

At the entrance
I receive a card
Become
For a time
Mrs. Frederick G. Quick,
Second class.

Before the voyage begins
I pass by the bunks
Of third class
(Better than second
On most ships)
To find my cabin.

After we embark
Oblivious to sweat in the boiler room
I notice the first-class ladies
In their sequined gowns.
Like a window shopper
In an upscale mall

I covet the blood diamonds
Heavy on their necks,
Admire their gold-edged dinnerware
And crystal flutes.
I even ascend
The grand staircase

And view the ballroom,
Hear strains of "The Merry Widow"
Oblivious to the ocean around me,
Like someone
Topping off his tank
During an oil spill in the Gulf.

On the last night
Stars erupt in a black sky
Like crystals
On a chandelier,
More stars
Than I have ever seen

Almost enough for officers
Oblivious as CEOs to see without binoculars
The field of icebergs, white ghosts rising
In jagged silhouettes while the waltz
Still glimmers from the ballroom.
Then I feel the bump.

Soon the boilers go out and we fight
To board scarce lifeboats. The band plays
"Nearer My God to Thee" before their instruments
Tumble into the North Atlantic
Like trees falling in a rainforest,
Water flowing through their tubes and valves.

Lights in portholes blaze
As the jewel of the White Star Line
Cracks in half and 46,000 tons
Go down. Ice crystals swirl, close in
On the vanishing hull.
Oblivious, I survive.

On Charles Whitman

August 1 was hazy.
Students ambled to their classes
In unwilling herds, books
Balanced on their hips.

Three blocks away
In our decrepit rooms
I struggled with a birthday cake
Butter icing melting in the heat.

Inside the Tower
Carrels bulged with sluggish grads.
Traffic inched in lazy ribbons
Down the Drag.

No one saw
The ex-Marine
Who took the elevator
Far as it would go.

Summer oozed through walls
Crept up furniture.
I put the cake
Inside the fridge.

He reached the observation deck
Unpacked deodorant and rifles
Ate some lunch.
No one saw

At first
The lazy puffs of smoke, or heard
Those dull reports
That sounded like a distant fireworks show.

No one made connection
Even when the passersby
Began to melt
Along the sidewalks

Or in front of cars
And smoke kept rising
From the Tower
In languid spirals

Almost festive, like the fumes
From blown-out candles
On a youngster's
Birthday cake.

They got it, finally.
Phones went off
In high electric screams
And sirens scattered noon.

Police cars raced
Along the streets
In frenzied lines
Like worker ants defending hills

Smashed by a giant mower.
I got a call
From someone penned
Inside the Co-op.

He told me
To take cover
Told me
What I knew.

By nightfall
Heat had drained the campus
As the moon rose indolent

Above the blistered trees.

The cake
Had hardened in the fridge
Too stiff, too cold
To touch.

At the World Trade Center

Somewhere in the desert, dawn comes late
And angles of the world begin to shift
In acrid billows of free-floating hate.

Twin fireballs bloom like giant poppies, fate
Of millions melted down, consumed. Hands drift
Somewhere. In the desert, dawn comes late

As reams of paper spin through light, gyrate.
Shall dervishes in white, they drop and lift,
In acrid billows of free-floating hate

While grimed firefighters plod through ruin, their gait
Slowed by the footsore dogs that whimper, sniff
Somewhere in the desert. Dawn comes late

Through crumpled girders, sirens, shouts, a spate
Of cell phones ringing in the labyrinth
On acrid billows of free-floating hate.

Now at the fuming crypt new mourners wait,
Light candles, listen for a breath, a gift.
Somewhere in the desert, dawn comes late
In acrid billows of free-floating hate.

Teaching Before the War

In a stuffy classroom
Students grapple with Gandhi
Stumble over soul-force
Try to pin passive resistance
On the page

Their voices rising
In an angry hum
Like Apaches droning in the desert
Rotors whirling sand
Into cities far away.

They can't follow him
On his long march
Hold the salt of Dandi
In their hands, feel the ocean
Lapping at their feet.

Instead they watch
Humvees inch down the ramps
Like giant locusts
Ml6s unloaded
From their crates

Laser sights fixed
Before they get on board
The Blackhawks
For another ride
Of the Valkyries.

New Fridge

My grandparents bought it during Viet Nam
When no one talked of anything but Tet.
They saved ten years to have this luxury
Ensconced it in our kitchen
Like an oracle. It brought forth
Myriad meals in a sweaty room,
Cooled our powdered milk and old roast beef
Thousands of miles

From those steamier jungles
Deadly green, drone of helicopters
Napalm blooming over palm trees.
We ate our meager suppers
Just before the nightly news
Roared through our living room,
Watched mudstained infantry
Plod over armchairs, dodging mines and tables

Fording rivers on our carpet.
Finally we heard the casualty reports.
Later we would stuff leftovers
Back into the cold, wedge wrinkled grapes
Into their chilled compartments,
The next night burrowing
Through shelves like tunnel rats
Searching something fit to eat.

After the war and a twenty-year tour
The oracle came to me, suffered
The slings and arrows of a weary grunt
Churning valiantly with doors left open,
Ice trays running over
Magnets on the front
Bearing doctors' cards
And past-due bills.

Today we have a new one
And it runs like a sleek cat,
Its motor a complacent purr
But now the talk is all Iraq
And Lebanon, deserts, roadside bombs,
And I pack fish sticks in the freezer
Like soldiers
In Humvees.

How to Stop War

Put Yo Yo Ma in every doorway
Pavarotti at each checkpoint
Perlman on the road to Kosovo
Or in Rwanda's thick green hills.

Let the hands of Artur Rubinstein
Float slowly over Belfast
Have Marsalis
Shoot cadenzas into Gaza.

When we fill the bores
Of AK 47s
With scores of Brandenburg concertos,
When we arm the Stealths with Mozart

No one will hear the voices
Calling them to blood. Remastered
They will find their families
Building ballads in the streets

See them tuning old guitars
Inside their tents
Chords shimmering
In Kabul's radiant dust

Rising
Past
The minefields
Into melodies.

Fire in the Sierras

Even now
Fifty years beyond
Mother wrenches me
From sleep, drags me
From my dreams of endless green
Frantic hands
Sheathing me in blankets
As we stumble over building blocks
Ram the playhouse
Race to the waiting car
A muffled rush to safety
Further down.

Even now
I smell
That night:
Charred fur of pumas
Eucalyptus stripped
To acrid threads. Smoke
Clings
To my hair
In morbid wreaths
Coats fingers
Face
Tongue

While death
Roars down the mountain
Like a starving giant
Swallows
Everything
In breathless gulps
An ecstasy in red
Billows up toward heaven
Down toward everything

We have, know, are,
Titanic playmate
Eager for a brawl.

Even now
When sleep drifts through me
Like a sodden rain
I wake at two or three
Scan cool darkness
As I watch
And listen
For that huge vermilion voice.

Chocolate

(To Jonah)

I still recall those dour December skies
The afternoon a mass of cold and clouds
Heaped over our small town in sullen mounds
Like oatmeal left to harden in a bowl.

Trudging home from school, we'd reach the door
Plod to the kitchen, sigh at warmth and light
Then gasp: Grandmother had begun to bake
For Christmas and the house was steamy fudge,

A giant artifact of chocolate.
That mocha scent embedded in the rugs
And drapes, dark fragrance rolled along the walls.
Rivulets trickled down the stairs and dripped

From chandeliers in sugary streams.
We ran from room to room to find the source
But she had finished for the day, the bowls
Washed clean. She never brought the cookies out

Of hiding until Christmas Eve, and so
We learned to hunt, to fail, at last to wait.
We never beat her to her secret cache,
Not once, until last spring when we unearthed

One rusted tin stashed on the highest shelf,
Its contents mummified between the sheets
Of foil and paper. When I touched the glaze
It crumbled to a fine mahogany sand

But then I caught the faintest scent, a trace
Of mocha cream, and suddenly it was
December. We were trudging home from school
Toward everything beneath those oatmeal skies.

Target Practice

Mother packed a Colt
Because she feared them,
Feared those midnight pilgrims
Stumbling through the tumbleweeds
Sweat dried on their backs
Like a second skin
A few tortillas in a sack.

And so she lined us up
Each Saturday
Tecate Mountain behind us
A fence line
Thirty feet in front,
Juice cans balanced
On each post.

No lunch until we shot them down
One by one
Bird's Eye logos
Centered in our sights
Heavy steel wobbly
In our hands
The trigger hard to squeeze

But we brought them down
One by one
Shot after shot
Bullets ricocheting off the barn
Casings in the hay
We brought them down
Until one day

We saw those others, thin as twigs
Weightless as leaves
Weaving over the cattle guard

Like drunks dizzy in the morning air.
I felt the gun
Fall
To my side.

For Mary

The old house seems the same.
I walk from room to room
Pick up familiar scents:
Polished wood, pungent pines outside

A trace of nutmeg, homebaked bread.
I think I'll see her
Down the hall
Or in the breezeway

Watering her Christmas cactus,
Mulling over recipes.
I wander finally
Into the basement

Damp walls a respite
From the heat
And find her battered Singer
Threaded, needle up

Ready to begin
Another dress or shirt.
She always said
It shocked her when she sewed

That needle moving up and down
In silver spurts,
The wheel a mild conductor
Shooting current to her hands.

I remember all the time
She spent down here
Climbing creaking stairs
At last to show

The newest blouse
She'd made
For someone's niece,
A blue silk suit

Curtains for the den
Her fingers red and tingling
From the misplaced power.
Finally I touch

The guide
Feel the briefest jolt
While nothing moves.
Then I know.

Storm

It all seems safe today,
The Seawall rising twenty feet
Above gray waves, teens on skateboards
Gliding down broad sidewalks
Toddlers dripping ice cream
Down their chins.

But I remember
Breathless August afternoons
Grandmother telling me again
About the hurricane
That finished Galveston
In 1900, took six thousand lives.

She, the Ancient Mariner
Who had a story to tell
Would seize my wrist
And I
The adolescent Wedding Guest
Would have to hear.

She would number all the friends
She'd lost that warm September day
When seas crushed everything
For thirty miles
Lives ended in a counterclockwise sweep,
The deadliest in history.

Sweat would bead up on her brow
Droplets gathering between her sagging breasts
And darkening her faded dress
As heat filled every room
And drifted up the stairs,
Our old clock ticking in the hall.

She rambled of the wagons, rooftops, children, cattle
Thrown into the Gulf like pebbles
Mansions lifted from their piers like toys
Horses swirling through fine parlors
In surrealist pageantry
And then the pyres on a sodden beach.

I would yawn
And think about my date
That night,
The last hours spent
In the back seat
Of a Mustang.

I knew nothing
Of the storms
Already brewing
In rooms of houses
Not yet built, of fires
Already set.

Today I'd seize her wrist
And she, the Wedding Guest,
Would have to hear.

Stroke

(for Jane Shindler Crow)

Her hand.
Her good right hand.
At the desk her pen was once
A scalpel, cursive cutting through
The paper, leaving dainty stencils
On the other side

Or hammering her baby grand
Pounding out her favorites
Hour on hour
Beating Bach
Chopin or Lizst
Into compliance.

That same hand
Could navigate a needle
Through the finest silk
Embroider anything
Monogram a blouse
Or finish off a French-cut suit

And when she stepped up to the podium
Gripping her white baton
The orchestra would snap
Into sharp focus
Even those who might have dropped
Notes in rehearsal, missed a pick-up, come in flat.

Today her fingers curl
Like embryos
On the sheet. She hears me crying
From my crib and fears
A land invasion by the Japanese.
Already they have bombed Pearl Harbor.

Now she's dressing for my wedding
Starts to sing, breaks off:
"*Adiós muchachos, compañeros de mi vida...*"
Worn out from this excitement,
She cradles her shriveled arm
Like the baby she is carrying

Wonders why she's in a wheelchair
With her victory garden gone to seed
When she has nothing to fear
But fear itself,
Certain that she'll be restored
To everything she's lost
And found.

For John Masefield

I have it too, that fever
For the sea. Longing
Draws me in, makes all things
Move and shimmer.
Sunflowers sway like ghosts
On gray-green stalks
Jellyfish throbbing on damp sand
Mosquitoes in a frenzy at my ears.

And color: everything somehow imported
Apricot and turquoise
Emerald and ivory
Moving in the hottest waltz
Through this opal afternoon.
I walk along the beach
Dollops of tar
On either foot.

Young men stride along
Faces streaked with sunblock
Like a horde of extras
Costumed as Comanches
On the warpath
In a John Wayne flick.
Wet dogs trot through surf, yelp at waves.
I wade out at last

Glad that I can move
Against the undertow,
Think of Mother
Strapped into her wheelchair
Cutting through the blue Pacific
In imaginary strokes, the part of life
She can remember.
Now she's waiting to be fed.

My words snap off
Beneath the waves
Like brittle filigree,
Or froth
From breakers
Sinking into sand.

E.B. White Remembered

I gaze with comfortable nostalgia
At the photo of my grandparents
Taken many Christmases ago,
Their celebration framed in oak.

At first, time fades.
They almost step into my living room
Abandon for a while
Their mildly comic pose:
My grandmother a shade too plump
For their Victorian loveseat,
Poinsettias left blooming
On the marbletop behind them
Shooting red bracts
From their iron-gray hair. She smiles
Like this year's prom queen, one hand
Resting on her lap, the other
Draped across Grandfather's muscled back.
He looks impish, almost laughing
At some secret joke
His jacket slightly rumpled,
Windsor knot awry.

But just above
Their flowered heads
I see a second photo,
This one of their grandsons
Then in nursery school. Those boys
Own a software enterprise today.
I now observe
Grandmother's swollen knees,
Her husband's hands
Gnarled like venerable trees.
My fingers stiffen
In an instant recognition

As my grandchild wakes, clamors
To be rescued from her crib
And suddenly
I'm framed in oak,
Banks of blood-red poinsettias
Sprouting from my head.

Piano

Mother bought it second-hand
A grimy spinet
Shoved behind a Steinway.

We installed it in the living room
And she would play for hours
A can of beer warming on the cheek block

Mazurkas and impromptus spinning
In a dusty cloud, eight-to-the-bar
Thumping in the works.

Chopin, Bach and Liszt
Sat on our vinyl chairs
Hurling scores at her

And marginal corrections,
Beethoven sometimes helping her
Play "Für Elise."

Then I took over
Struggled through the Bach inventions
Sometimes a polonaise.

Soon children and grandchildren
Pounded it, chipped the keys
Kicked the soundboard.

One child stuffed a toy dog
Into the action. Finally
The cover wouldn't close. I called

The tuner. He brushed off
Fifty years,
Cleaned the hammers. Suddenly

Bars of "Für Elise"
Jumped from the keyboard,
Strains of Mozart

Floating upward from the pedals
And I almost saw
My mother

Thumbing scores and turning pages
Hunting for the perfect piece
A warm beer in her hand.

A Young Doctor
(for Ruth)

She'll need wings on her feet
The speed of serpents
And a wand in her hand
Like Mercury
To walk the thousand miles
That soon will fill her life.

She'll wear a white coat now,
Her name emblazoned on the pocket
Like a talisman.
A stethoscope will dangle
From her neck
Like a fifth appendage

As she hears the muffled heartbeats
Swoosh of the mother seas
First wails
And final syllables
Drifting through a galaxy
Of rooms,

Her ears always alert
For the pager in the night.
Her hands will coax new life
From aching portals
And she'll learn to say
"Es un niño. Todo está bien"

Twenty times a week.
A benevolent Hydra
She'll grow new lives
With every year,
Ulysses in the operating room,
A part of everything she meets:

The luminous newborn
An octogenarian with a broken hip
Another with a leaky mitral valve
Someone's rasping breath
But always
At the center

She will live in miracles unnamed
Like the imperial koi
Floating silently in their pool
Beneath a willow tree
Each green leaf
Still above green water.

Tattoo

(for Adam)

My face is burned into my son
At twice life size
Shades of ochre, flame and blue.
I think of needles, dyes
The artist saying things like "Raise your arm,"
"Keep still" or "Good work isn't cheap.
Cheap work isn't good"
While he extracts
From muscle
Curls and bright coronas
Set around my face

But not my face
Not my features now
Their contours drooping into time.
Instead the artist works in memory
A crinkled photograph
Taken thirty years ago
When I was first engaged.
I smile into the future
Knowing nothing that would come
Backlight shooting rays
Into my new-permed hair.

The face that slowly surfaces
Beneath the needle
Is not mine
But his
Those untried bones, taut lines.
The artist adds another swirl
And we are canonized
My son and I
Unlikely sainthood
Radiant

Along his spine.

I ponder this apotheosis.
My face then
Is his face now, his is mine
Replicated in the visage
I once had.
I see my days
Now moving in reverse.
We lose time and recover it
Lose it again in double progress
Sooner, later, sweeping both of us
Beyond the picture.

Birthday

(for Emily Caroline)

Almost iridescent
Underneath the lights
Her body shimmering
Like mother of pearl
She opens her new eyes
To moving shadows
Large gloved hands, a mass of wires
And screens, small ears picking up
The gasps and sobs
Like an explorer
Taking on new continents
Finding the terrain
In sound and touch.

Waking from one dream
Of life into the next,
Already she contains
A hundred songs
That she will sing
Steps to dances by the dozen,
Music from the now lost sea
Floating in her cries
Pictures forming in the contours
Of her glossy hands,
Moments that will sear her
Freeze her
Growing in some other room.

A luminous voyager
Transplanted
From her old familiar place
Into a mystery,
She starts to shape
Her space and time

Even when the doctor
Cuts her lifeline
And she reaches out, alone,
To learn the unknown land.

Replay

My grown son stands in the goal again
Back at soccer after all this time.
He slams the ball
Across midfield or into a corner
Leather at tight angles
Edging it past opposing forwards
Sailing it over their heads
Like a parabolic thought.

Muscular and rowdy,
Caught up in this ballet for jocks
Chess on grass,
He shouts at his teammates
As he did twenty years ago
Gripes at the ref
As he did twenty years ago
Makes a save,
The ball surrenderlng
To his gloved hands.

I think of the chlld he was
Of the man who coached him
His hands on my son's hands
Showing him gently
How to grip the ball
How to trap it
Hurl it into heaven
In spinning arcs
Bury it
In a furious embrace.

My son is studying law these days
Poring over torts
Life less a game
But for the moment

He's a child
And I am young again
Watching for his next great save
Waiting for a furious embrace.

Election Day, 2008

Who would have believed
In Lincoln's bloody land
Places where nooses
Hung from giant oaks
Like alien Spanish moss
That such a thing could be?

Who would have guessed
Where sharecroppers in cotton fields
Lived and died on molasses and mush
While others froze in miles of crumbling brick
Broken glass and free-range rats
That such a time could come?

Who would have thought
So many could travel
Down paths worn smooth by night-riders
Past burning crosses, water fountains
And polling places out of reach
To find a place in the front of the bus?

Yet on this day
A jubilee began: hymns rolled down like rivers
From the fire hoses, dreams rose
From the muzzles of rifles, flowers sprouted
Out of manacles
And all the police dogs
Bayed hallelujah
In a chorus no one will forget.

For a New Grandchild
(to Cash)

When you began
All the trees were electric green.
Their voltage charged the city
Levitating leaves
On dusty streets.

Mountain laurels
Bloomed their purple songs
And redbuds sprouted arias
By dumpsters.

Open egg shells
Dotted grass
Like oversized confetti.
Unseen fledglings
Chirped across the sky

While in a quiet room
You lay,
A tranquil cipher
Small Buddha, inscrutable
With dimples and a bloody head.

Wars stopped.
Poisons vanished from the earth and sea.
No one went hungry. All ate well
And for one day
The world was made anew.

Family Gathering

In my dream
I'm looking at a crinkled photo
Taken Easter Sunday
In an unknown year.
Faces come into sharp focus
Vanish, reappear
In endless rounds.
Fade in
Fade out.

Mother hasn't had her stroke
Or is that Grandmother
With the tired blue eyes, her veined arms
Wrapped around a great-grandchild
Who's just learned how to walk?
Is that my daughter's baby? Mine?
My sister is still pregnant
With a second girl,
Or is that child a boy? Her first or third?

Now I'm in the picture.
Caught between these overlapping lives
I show off
A yellow linen suit,
Stand with my son
And his new girlfriend.
Lilies drift in random progress
Past the frame. Fade in,
Fade out.

Brothers, husbands join us,
Stare responsibly into the lens
But now it's 1943.
My father, a Marine, cradles me
While I squall at the top of my new lungs

And his mother leaves off
Building fighter planes
To smile at us admiringly.
Or is that man my son?

I want to walk out of this portrait
And its decades floating by
In blurry pageants
But the others pull me back
Into their shimmering tableaux
Of love
And loss
Played through uncertain light.
Fade in, fade out.

Book Club Discussion Questions

1. What is the significance of the title? In what way (s) might it apply to the entire work?

2. "At the World Trade Center" (p. 143) is a villanelle, a form requiring rigid rhyme and repetition. How does the use of these devices affect the poem's rhetorical impact?

3. Members of the author's family figure prominently in many of these poems. Which strike you as most memorable? Why?

4. "On Charles Whitman" (p.140) is a retelling of the UT-Austin Tower shooting of 1966, an event which the author witnessed. How does she characterize Whitman? What personality emerges from the details she includes?

5. Although the author was born in California, she is an adopted Texan who writes frequently about the Lone Star State. What vision of Texas does she convey in her poetry? Is that view primarily positive or negative? Give examples to support your response.

6. "One Night in a Cheap Motel" (p.131) pays homage to T.S. Eliot's "The Love Song of J. Alfred Prufrock" and draws heavily on allusions to Eliot's famous portrait of a man who doubts his manhood. Read Eliot's poem and then examine the use of allusions in Reposa's poem. How many do you find? Does the ending of "One Night in a Cheap Motel" suggest an outcome different from that implied in Eliot's poem?

7. The poems comprising the Elizabeth I sequence (pp. 39-48) are sonnets, a form requiring the use of iambic pentameter, a rigid rhyme scheme, and an equally rigid pattern of organization. In a sense, sonnets are verbal straitjackets. What is gained by the use of this form? What is lost? Support your answer with reference to specific poems.

8. "Galápagos Soap Opera" (p.26), "Bathing (p.56), "Proposition" (p.80), "At Peterhof" (p.84), and "Multi-Tasking" (p.126) treat life humorously. Discuss sources of humor in one or more of these poems. What people, places, and events strike the author as funny?

9. "At Shakespeare's Birthplace" (p.38), "Lines Composed in the Computer Classroom" (p.116), "Multi-Tasking" (p.126), "Town Homes in Houston" (p.132), and "At the World Trade Center" (p.143) mention technological devices. What does the author think of them? Include specific examples in your discussion.

10. Which of the many historical figures portrayed in this book would you most like to meet? Which would you like to avoid? Why?